# HIGHER MOTIVATION VOL. 1

# HIGHER MOTIVATION
# VOL. 1

## "LYRICAL. LIFE. LESSONS."

WRITTEN AND THOUGHT OUT IN ENTIRETY
BY: AA'SHIA D. JACKSON

XULON PRESS

Xulon Press
2301 Lucien Way #415
Maitland, FL 32751
407.339.4217
www.xulonpress.com

Unless otherwise indicated, Scripture quotations taken from the King James Version (KJV) – *public domain.*

Paperback ISBN-13: 978-1-6628-2433-3
Ebook ISBN-13: 978-1-6628-2434-0

## "A Mental Note"

WE CAN ONLY GO AS FAR AS OUR MINDS CAN TAKE US. HOW FAR HAVE WE PREPARED OUR MINDS TO GO? THE ONLY THINGS THAT TRULY EXIST TO A PERSON ARE THE THOUGHTS THAT LIVE INSIDE OF THEIR MIND. PEOPLE HAVE BUILT UP THEIR OWN FICTIONAL WORLD TO LIVE IN. ONE WHERE EVERYTHING WORKS AROUND THE WAY THAT THEY FEEL AND THEIR THOUGHTS TEND TO DETERMINE OR DETER THEM. THE WAY ONE THINKS CAN MAKE OR BREAK THEM IN THIS WORLD WE LIVE IN. REALISTIC THINKING IS ALWAYS THE BEST WAY TO GO. HOWEVER, BE WITHIN REASON! THE MAJORITY OF OUR THOUGHTS ARE LED BY OUR FEELINGS AND OR EMOTIONS. OUR EMOTIONS ARE WHAT GUIDE US AND WE BELIEVE IT IS OUR RIGHT: TO JUDGE, OPINIONIZE, AND ACT ON THEM WHENEVER WE SEE FIT. WE ARE WRONG! WE NEED TO ALLOW OUR CREATOR TO GUIDE US AND BE MORE IN TUNE WITH THE SCRIPTURE TO THEREFORE UNDERSTAND AND THUS BE ABLE TO MOBILIZE AND MOVE ABOUT IN THIS WORLD WITHOUT BEING A TARGET FOR DISRUPTION. THIS GUIDE IS

FOR MENTAL NOTES, BUT NOT FOR EVERYTHING IN YOUR LIFE TO BE SOLELY BASED UPON. IN ORDER TO DO THAT YOU WILL NEED THE HOLY BIBLE. ALLOW ME TO GUIDE YOU THERE, TO THE TRUTH THAT WAS PREVIOUSLY WRITTEN. HIGHER MOTIVATION/ LYRICAL LIFE LESSONS IS STRICTLY A CHECKPOINT OR BREAK DOWN OF UNDERSTANDING YOUR TRUE CHARACTER. TAKE IT FOR WHAT YOU WILL AND LET US BUILD. TOGETHER WE CAN GET THERE. -Ai'scei Gold'n Babei

# TABLE OF CONTENTS

# "Spiritual Realm"

S ome people are just alive but are not conscious of the spiritual realm that surrounds them. There are vapors or airs amidst us, and their circular levels surround us. We cannot necessarily see them. What I do know is that good or bad, things of this world cling onto our spiritual realm every day. We are not even aware of it when it is occurring. Everything that you have been introduced to becomes a part of you in some shape, form, or fashion. From the day you are conceived, you begin soaking up the nature around you. You start coming into your own realizations of your pure and impure likes and dislikes. You begin associating yourself with the things that interest you. But all this interest has come from everything that has surrounded you, or that you have encountered since the beginning of your life. You start picking up on comforts, bad habits, and moreover characterized behavior.

Let us discuss comforts for a moment. Comforts are the things that feel natural to you, or the things that make you conform to them without any outside assistance. We will almost always revert to our comforts because they are what is most known to us. These can be simple things like home, or a loved one; it could also be music, or any outlet that allows us to re-adjust ourselves in any situation. All these things are a part of our spiritual realms, and they can be either beneficial or detrimental to progression in our life. Sometimes we must take a step outside of our comforts. If we allow them to over-populate our spiritual realms, we will find ourselves never growing. Lean not unto your own understanding because one will never reach their fullest potential, there will always be room for growth. Never get so comfortable or complacent that you become satisfied with any current state, and always seek knowledge because a mind is a powerful thing to waste. Remember that even your comforts can hurt you. No individual, human being, or any other living organisms, of this world, will last forever.

Therefore, nothing of this world is worth that much of your devotion. The only spiritual being, essence, and everything that is truly real eternally is God. If we put half as much effort into the transformation of ourselves for our God to be pleased with us, as we do in conforming to our own comforts, we would get at least two times the results in life.

Habits are something that we all pick up. They can be both good and bad. Good habits are great to take on, especially if it includes a righteous way of living. We must try not to pick up too many bad habits because they are hard to kick, or to get rid of once they are picked up. Bad Habits come from several things, but curiosity and influence are number one. Being able to be afflicted or affected in this way is not a good thing. It shows signs of weakness. Everything is either spiritual, physical, or mental. The world can lead us astray if we allow it. If we are worried about keeping up with the majority then this is the wrong thing to be worried about. We need to cleanse our spiritual realm of bad habits, no matter what they are. Habits can form comforts, but habitual bad behavior will eventually cause a shut-down. You will run into some type of wall. They could even cause you to lose your life. When the bad habits get into our spiritual realm, they can sometime determine who we are, or who we have become. They can also change us and re-create a new demeanor. Everyone can see it occurring but the eye of the beholder, and it is much easier to tell someone else what they need to do regarding their lives, as opposed to what we should be doing with our own lives. This type of hypocritical behavior can be critical. It all stems back to self-control. What is so wrong with doing what is right?

Characterized behavior is when someone creates a whole new identity for themselves and begins to live and portray the character in mind. This fictional characterized behavior starts in the mind. Think about a musician. Musicians create a new name, a new image, a new persona. If the musician had the opportunity to travel and live the glamorized life that comes along with it, then the musician would have known what it is to have a life on the stage. That musician would have known a life that is staged. A life that becomes you, and clings onto your spiritual realm. We must be careful with nicknames and labels. One can really begin to take on the characteristic of the basic meaning of the nickname, and they themselves begin to lose the real them in the process. The individual may want to be always addressed by their nickname. They may even ask that family members, and loved ones, who have known them all their lives, address them as such. But do you think that this is a bit much? Have you put that much more focus into the real you? As soon as we are disappointed in our make-believe lives, we want to revert to the real us. But times get harder in doing so because it has been so long since we have been the real us, that no treats us the same. They make call you fake, or claim that you forgot where you came from, but it could be because you never understood where you were going!

The key to cleansing your spiritual realm, whether it is of comforts, bad habits, or characterized behavior, is to always stick to the facts and be true to oneself. If we utterly understood what the things, we allow ourselves to consume could do to us, we would eliminate a whole lot of comforts and bad habits. Also, if we change our way of thinking to the way of thinking, then we will begin to see everything in life from a more solid perspective and there definitely would be no need for characterized behavior. If you understood who you were, you would absolutely love yourself and would not want to be anyone other than the real you. None of the non-sense would serve as relevance. If we could all just take a good look at the life that the Most High laid out for us, we would see that it really does not get any better. Everything that we place our trust, love, desire, energy, and time into was not designed with our feelings in mind. We must know this and embrace growth. Because whether we know it or not, the best way to gain an attachment to the Most High, is to have a spiritual realm attached to nothing of this world.

# "Bringing About Division"

T here happens to be a division line for every aspect of life. This includes the good, the bad, the right, the wrong, life, death, blessings, or curses. Do you believe everything happens for a reason? Do you believe in your sound judgment? Let us re-evaluate ourselves. Are we on the realer aspect of life or the fake? Making this decision, and living it, will determine every-thing that our lives will become. Some things just never change as we know, but often we still have a chance at improving the outcome of our lives. The Most High will take us through many paths to reach our destinations in this life. How do we know what is real? We allow the prophecy of the Holy Bible to guide us as we are living. Every day we feed our spirits with the right things, and more and more we will begin to live it, to breathe it, as it is our natural nature. There are some who choose to enter-tain the wrong things and have lost their way or never knew their way, there are many who conquer joy through doing the wrong things, and then there are those who choose life, and understand what it means to be living as opposed to just alive.

You should know that there are quite a few people surrounding you that have no clue what is going on. They have no under-standing of what is real. These are people who have been caught up instead of being brought up on wisdom. Some people do not have the ability to think with a divisive mind. It is because they do not understand what is happening in this life. As far as they know, life is a gamble, you smile and you cry, you live, and you die. It is as simple as this for some. But what if I told you there was no such thing as luck, or that everything either happens because it is meant to happen, or does not occur because it is not meant to occur that way? Life is not a gamble; life is distinctly designed. What has been prophesied on, is coming to pass, and some people have no clue, no knowledge of reality. They often live at standstills, with no knowledge of why they are not being blessed to progress. Is it because they have yet to decide what side they are on? Or is it because they entertain, and lend their ear to the wrong things? Do not get me wrong; at one point or another, we have all been there! But the key is to find you. The key is to grow upward and to begin to entertain the right things at some point. Is there really a point to going to church and reading along like you are truly Intune, and then leaving just be possessed, or taken by whatever confronts you. This type of hypocritical behavior can prove to be critical. The things of this world were all put here to throw you off or knock you off your focal point. Not one thing, but the spirit of the Most High, are we strong enough to obtain without being swayed by worldly ways. The flesh is weak, and susceptible to all sorts of things. Most individuals are trying, will try anything at least once in their life and will entertain almost anything. People get caught up on the glamour and the make- up that the world wears. Everything that looks good is not always! We must all have a way of life about ourselves. We cannot just continue to go with the flow, follow all the newest trends, submit self to crews, cliques, fraternities, and secret societies, without having knowledge of oneself. How can we take oath to the world without even giving the Creator an opportunity to reveal the truth to us? Have we chosen a side, and do we know if we are serving the Most High or the fallen angel? Many individuals still have a chance to obtain a relationship with the God. All that is needed to do is awaken the conscious and feed the spirit with the right combination of knowledge, confidence, and determination.

There is a more down- sided- side, however. Do not forget, there are individuals around every minute, of every hour, who love to be rebellious. They love to do the wrong things, and pursue others to do the wrong things, as well. Misery loves company. Some people have made up their minds that they will not do what is right, but only the things that feel right to them. They have accepted the world as their own personal savior and placed their trust into it. Do not sleep for a moment believing we are all confused, or unconscious. This is not the case. Some individuals have deceptive ways about them, and they are a part of another entity. They do not fear the Lord and have not accepted the only Begotten Son into their hearts as their savior. They are also a part of a plan for destruction. They wish to obtain the respect from all but refuse to give it in return. They walk about, making up deceptive stories, and using their manipulative ways to force others into the ways of deceptiveness. Just remember that these people are conscious of what they are doing, and they have no regard for the Most High, Creator of all things. Never follow a fool because they live life according to their emotions and have little self-control. They do not fear the Lord and are not willing to change. Their destiny and destination are already set. Everyone should want to be blameless in the eyes of the Lord and these people are alive and well, breathing and recruiting an army for the devil. They live amongst the few righteous. If we are one who has not found our way, then we should be extremely cautious around individuals like this. The flesh is weak, and we are not all playing for the same team. When we say that we love the Lord, we must know it and be prepared to show it. This may mean sacrificing the emotions of the flesh for the intent of the spirit. We must show and prove. The Most High put something inside of us all, and we all fit together a certain way to complete the puzzle of life. Be cautious of praising someone, or something other than the God. Remember that God created all things, both great and small, as well as both man, and beast, so choose wisely when you decide which side you are on. How could the Most High ever be defeated by one of his very own creations? Who will you serve: creation, or Creator?

If we are choosing life, then we are choosing to pursue a god-like life form of mannerism. If we are simply choosing to be alive, then all we have decided is that you are living, as opposed to dead with the option of being alert and active when deciding to. Gain an understanding of what is real. You may not know it all, but at least your mind is open to growth, and your heart is open for healing. All we must do is embrace what is real and stop making everything as hard as it seems or could appear to be. We must stop making excuses and start making decisions. By building in the Holy script, we can learn to fear nothing but the Lord, and by doing so, we gain our shield, or our protection from this world.

At that point, we should no longer be affected anymore. We should finally be able to open our eyes and devise. To smell a skunk before our eyes know it is a skunk, and to read between the lines while sharpening our edges up. With a keen sense of judgment, one can decipher right from wrong. This society has made it acceptable to do the wrong things, and to glorify this. But a righteous mind has the ambition and drive to do what is right. This is a stage of maturity, of understanding, or growth. Once we have reached this stage in life, it will automatically bring about division. The reason is because the real separate themselves from the fake through everyday encounters and actions. When we are Intune spiritually, the higher self will pick up on things quickly and we can vibe off spiritual realms that surround people. This is a part of the intuition God instilled within us all. We tend to have a keener sense of judgment. You become vigilant, and heedful in your ways. Being spiritually Intune helps us to understand visitation, the visitation of a blessing or the visiting of affliction. We also realize that more and more people may turn against us; may act as though they themselves hate us. This is because they too realize what is inside of us, and somehow, they must excel above that to make themselves look and feel better, but the ones entertaining it are just as caught up as them, or worse because they are followers of iniquity and not just doers of iniquity, as we all are at times.

To sum this chapter up, basically we all have attributed to the loss of the real way, or our true alignment, and or true plan for our lives. Are duty being to be leaders of a righteous way of living, born into this world with a specific identity and purpose. "We all are like pieces to a puzzle; we fit a certain way, and I do believe that 'the purpose of life is to have a life of purpose'." Everything that occurs is necessary; the most important thing to understand is that this is not our story to tell. It is His-Story, or history and either way it is the Most High's story to tell. We cannot attempt to distinguish our own understanding; we must lean unto the understanding of our Father, Our Creator, and his only begotten son! All praise should be given unto thee, and not unto ourselves. This as well poses a problem. We see through our own eyes, and we conquer with our own hands and minds, but we forget to give the glory and praise to our Creator: the one and only who made all things possible. We have those who just live, and then they die without a true understanding of what the purpose of their existence ever was. We were all put here with a purpose. There were many who did not make it here but were on their way...think about it. When we live a rebellious life, that is what you get out of life, rebellion. When we live a disrespectful life, that is what you get out of life, disrespect. We cannot resist authority of the ultimate Law. We are in the Last Days. Read the Scriptures because we too should know the truth, and we cannot obtain it from another individual of this world.

# "Just Put It Down"

Now it is time we look at the aspect of self-control, and what causes us to become out of control beings. We as human beings take on a whole lot dealing with this world and the people that we meet daily. We meet, we greet, and we get chuckled in and obligate ourselves to the lives of others. I am speaking on people we let into our lives by our own free will. The Most High will oftentimes put people in our lives as a blessing, but all visitations are not a blessing. Some people are there to strictly knock us off our course. We attach ourselves to the wrong things, and instead of attaching ourselves to our Creator, we attach ourselves to people of this world who make the same mistakes that we do. Instead of placing our trust and understanding in our Creator, we place our trust and understanding into people of this world that lack understanding like we do. There is a huge problem here. Guess what? That person we love so dearly does not understand. Guess what we have? You have another unstable human being; a human being unstable to the point where you could never trust them, because they cannot guarantee themselves. They will always let you down, and so just put it down. Now is the time that we eject certain trusts, standards, and upholds for these people out of our mental. In the end it will only bitter you. You must focus on what makes you stronger and channel into you. Really focus!

There will be many tests, trials, and tribulations. The test will be subjecting to conditions that disclose the true character of someone in relation to what the Most High wishes for them to be, the trial will be your examination before our Father for the facts of the Law, and the tribulation will be the condition of affliction, distress, and long suffering that we will endure if we do not stop worrying about the wrong things.

Every day is a constant test. We can learn something new without an attempt. We as a human race are not focused. We have not figured out what it is truly about; what we are here for. We waste time, and put focus into those things that fall short and leave us with another unproductive day. Another day gone, but did we allow this day to prepare us for what awaits tomorrow, or did we allow this day to be adulterant; corrupt by a mixture of ingredients; a mixture of people, lies, and disruptive non-sense? That would be a complete waste of a day, and a waste of our mind's day after day! We go through tests to get better and so it is alright if we all fall short sometimes, because we have not failed yet; it is not over. We have yet to arrive at our individual trials, or our examination before the Lord. While we have an opportunity to make things right, to show and prove, to be productive; to set down the foolishness: the boyfriends, the girlfriends, the promiscuity, the drama, the love for the fast life, we should. Time waits for not a one of us. Everything that we truly desire in our hearts, which we seek for, the God would provide to us if we would just abide in Him. We just must put everything else down. All that we want will come if you just be patient and wait on the Lord!

Some of you reading this may not exactly understand the afterlife. You may not understand that what you do here in this life is preparation for the afterlife. First, there is only one way, and it is that of the Lord! It cannot be duplicated nor re-established. The Law of the Lord is already established; and our souls are headed somewhere whether we know it or not. Who have you given your soul to? Who have you offered your life to? Have we truly given our lives to our Creator, or are we seeking blessings from another entity? Who are we praying to? Surely this is a concern. How do you live against the will of the Most High everyday and still receive blessings from Him? I believe that you must abide in the will of the Lord one hundred percent in order to truly reap the benefits of what the Lord has for you, and that at that point and time you must be willing and ready to receive it. This truth can only be found through devotion and meditation of His Torah. So, does it make you wonder how one can get so far along in this world doing the all the wrong things, and another can struggle for so long doing all the right things? Well, that goes back to reading The Script. You would know that we were cursed because we did not listen to the voice of our God and will still do not.

We were chosen to be the Most High's people, and him our God. How does it make us look following the ways of the heathens and we are God's people? The end of the Gentile rule is coming, and the beginning of the New Holy Jerusalem follows. We are a stiff-necked people; the Bible tells us this. Affliction was placed on us because of this. We were to suffer in this life because of our ways. I am not saying that you cannot be blessed in this world, but you must be on a righteous path. These people reaping the benefits of the glamour, the money, and the fame are selling their souls. Some of these individuals are conscious and others are not. There is no way to be against God and be blessed by Him all at the same time. A trial awaits us all; it is the day when we must face our Maker. The truth will reveal itself for us all! We are all workers of iniquity, but this must change before it is too late! Just remember no one knows the date, nor the hour of their departure and time waits for no man nor woman. Take heed and place the Scripture into your stride, as it part of you. Allow it to become you and live-in purity. For only one-third of us all will truly be saved!

Take a good look at Joshua Chapter 1 and pay attention to what the Most High told Joshua, and how Joshua responded concerning his duties that the Most High had commanded of him. Not only that, but how his army responded as well. Read the words of the Messiah himself in John Chapter 5:19-47 and John 6:22-65 and read on to hear about how the Most High does not hear sinners Chapter 9:1-41.

# "Be Strong And Courageous"

The human anatomy is somewhat like the anatomy of a plant. We must water our lives for them to grow. There is a process of decomposition for us all; a point where we begin to break down into a simpler form. From that of which we arrived; we shall depart. If we continue to feed our temples with the wrong food, the wrong substances, and the wrong knowledge, we will continue to attribute to our own processes of decomposition. We need to animate our lives to be more vivacious. There were natural cures that the Most High put right here on this earth, but we do not know of them because all we do is live for today. No understanding of the past to see how we could even arrive to this point now and no understanding of our preparation for tomorrow. No knowledge. We continue to poison our bodies with the food that has been altered. We continue to poison our bodies with drugs and alcohol, knowing the effect of them. And we continue day after day without a clue of where we came from, what we are here for, and where we are headed now! We are living dangerously. In these last days we must be strong and courageous! Sometimes it can be hard to go against the grain, or what we have become used to, but we must keep our temples upright.

The foods of this world have been defiled, just as we have; from the pork (which we should not eat) to the beef and chicken as well. Do you not believe we as a people have been brainwashed and poisoned? Would it not be safe to say that the animals we eat have been defiled as well? The spirits of dead carcass that we feed our temples are defiled, and more than likely demonic spirits. It is hard to trust anyone or anything these days, but whatever happened to growing your own produce? People have gotten lazy, and that is exactly what is killing us all. Most people would rather go out to eat at a fast-food restaurant chain than to cook for themselves. It seems to be a faster and more efficient way to be fed, however, this is the main source of obesity in this country. Not only are we attributing to the growing percentage of fat in our bodies, but we are also poisoning ourselves. America is all about population control. The fast-food chain is another convenient way to kill us all. The government of this country knows exactly what their intent is. Just look at the calorie percentage of any menu at any burger joint in this country. You may not know, but it reads death at an early age, and half the time you are not even being given real meat.... real beef, real chicken, real fish, or real pork. Would you believe you may have even eaten cloned meat? It is hard to live in a place where you cannot trust the people feeding you, but it is true. Fruits and vegetables were designed to keep the body healthy, energized, and strong. Really, we could survive on them alone with water, of course. The things that can be grown from the earth, that the Most High put right here, in the beginning in the purest form, must be good for you. It was what was intended, and in a time where the animals of this world were non- corrupt, they were good for you. The Holy Bible tells us of such things we should not eat, and we have made them apart of our everyday choices. Whether you want to believe it or not, there are foods that heal and foods that kill. As we get older, we start eating our fruits and vegetables more. They become apart of our appealing taste buds, and we begin to understand a little more about what they can do for us. It is important as a parent to ensure that your children are eating the right things early in life. This way, they will grow up already in the format of eating the foods that are healthy for them, and they will learn to love them.

Now you can probably guess what I am going to say about drugs, but it is more than likely because we all know that they are no good for anyone or anything. Drugs alter your mind, your thinking, and your state of being. Why would anyone want to do something that made them a completely different person unless they had issues with their character at first? First thing we must begin to do is embrace and love our Creator, so that we can understand to love ourselves. There is much to understand about us all. We are creations of the Most High! And something special was put inside of us all. People experiment with drugs and other substances for several reasons... but it all boils down to knowing yourself. We must want to treat ourselves better and eject the mind-state of "what ever feels good." All that glitters is not gold. Just because the world is corrupt does not mean that we must be vile right along with it. I mean how silly can people be. Just think about cigarettes, they basically tell you what will happen to you if you smoke them, and people still do. Or even the effects of crack cocaine. We have all seen someone who smokes crack or uses a form of the substance itself in action. They make a fool of themselves and lower the likeness of all the people who ever knew them. Heroin users cannot even be communicated with because they are sleeping or nodding off every other second. And alcohol, well we have all seen what alcohol does to one, especially if their tolerance for the substance is low. Drugs make people look and act silly. We are only bringing ourselves down by ignoring the fact of the truth. We should always do the right things, and when we choose to entertain the wrong things, it is a disgrace to our culture. Look at how the Most High's children move about. We do not even love our Creator enough to love ourselves. We must do more positive things to build ourselves up, whether it be mentally, spiritually, or physically.

Our knowledge is the key to our understanding and success in this life. It is also the key to understanding everything covered in this entire book. You see, we as a people have allowed ourselves to get entirely too far from the truth. Knowledge is will always be power and the keep to leading a prosperous life. Now a day, people do not exercise their minds, and they simply allow themselves to soak up a million and one so-called truths. This has led to a big misunderstanding. Seeking knowledge for self is the best thing we can ever do because it allows us to see things for fact and not opinion. It all goes back to perspective. Ten different people will see the same exact thing ten different ways. Everyone telling their story has seen life from a completely different angle, and not only that, but we were all built in diverse ways. Therefore, we will all see driven by what makes us who we are. We are built up on emotion, spirit, and flesh, and this varies with each person. We are all different. You cannot even get two identical people with identical twins. But knowledge is in the eye of the beholder. You must take it for what you will. If we do receive a hint of knowledge from another individual of this world, we must first check it out and do our research. Remember that all knowledge coming from another individual is self-driven by their own individual thoughts, emotions, and opinions. The usage of knowledge given by another individual reflects their own biases, and somewhat makes you look silly because the people that truly know you can see that what you are speaking on is not coming from you.

Never be afraid to go against the grain of this society because it is not built up around purity. If you are a spiritual person, then you will understand that you cannot be of this world, and one should not be full of pridefulness. There is a guide for living, and your instructions can be found within The Holy Bible. All that you are required to know is inside of it and the individual that it builds you up to be is remarkable. You cannot obtain that being someone of this world, nor can you obtain it from someone of this world. You must search deep within you. You must study to acquire the level of knowledge that you wish to obtain! It takes perseverance and determination; or just simply the desire to want more out of life. We just need to be more consciously aware and decide if we want to lead healthy or destructive lives. Whether it is concerning the foods we consume, or the drugs and knowledge we allow ourselves to squander.

# "Understanding Yourself Is Key"

P eople are so distinctive. There is much to understand about us all. Now is the time that we begin to analyze, conceptualize, and prioritize. Channeling into ourselves may seem hard to do, but it is as simple as the slogan for Nike, "Just Do It." Take time out to yourself with the opinion of no one else around, but the truth and the realities of the God's word. This is called ejection, direction and then protection. The ejection of the worldly evaluation from the mind of another individual, the direction from the Holy Script to gain a sense of understanding who we are and what purpose we truly serve, and the protection of knowing that if we lead a successfully righteous and healthy life that we are girded from the ways of the world. Instruction must be followed because it has been given. Things really are not as complicated as they seem. People complicate their own lives. Quite ironic how people find simple ways to complicate situations. Still, they have no understanding of simplicity. Life could be a breeze if we took out the time to channel into ourselves to gain a better understanding of who we are. For this is the true key to simplicity.

First thing we must do is eject useless people, emotions, and materials out of our lives and admit our spiritual realms. Number one thing to be ejected is useless emotions because they lead us to the feelings that we endure for useless people and materials. Be aware that the things of this world are not completely what they seem to be. One must make preparation for let downs when trust and understanding is placed into things of this world. Everything is an illusion, a mirage, except that of the truth. Be in search of THE TRUTH not A TRUTH! The truth never changes, but we must conform to fit ourselves into it. Ejection is a great thing! This does not mean that we must be alone. It simply suggests that we become more in-tune with who we are, and the number one way to accomplish this is to eject the opinions of others out of the mental, as it applies to us. Know thy Creator, so that you may know thy self. This will ensure that relevance drives you wherever one insists to take you. This is a key to simplicity. It is too much of a hassle to listen to everyone else when it comes to finding the solution to anything. Always remember to ask yourself first. At least you are closer to the truth that way. You are only one step away from knowing it for sure. The next step is to refer to The Script so that you may find the real answer. If you took the knowledge, or lack thereof, from someone else, you would still have to ask yourself, and then refer to the real source. Think about it, those are three steps as opposed to two. Why not just answer it for yourself and check your own thinking? We must change our process of thinking so that our lives can be made simpler. The key is to work smarter not harder. Life really is not as hard as it seems. Ejection is like cleansing the spiritual realm in a way. It is like having a new chance at becoming a new person. A person not built by the perception of others. The true test of character is based on the perception of everything tangible to oneself in relation to oneself and what he or she may or may not be able to acquire in this life.

We all need a little direction. Direction is the point toward which we are headed. Direction can also be our instructions. We could all get ahead if we got a head. Direct oneself attention to The Holy Script if you have not done so already. The truth can be obtained through it, along with gazing into oneself. The most important thing to understand is that we must try to understand all things as much as we can, and as far as our minds will take us. We do no justice for ourselves by creating our own truths, or beliefs. The best thing that we can do is embrace the truth because it cannot be re-designed. In fact, the truth has been designed for a specific purpose. We need it for everlasting survival. The Script teaches us to gird up, and to be knowledgeable about all things occurring, and it allows us to have a preparative mind, or a definite keen mind able to decipher the truth from the works. We should all have a sense of direction, even if we do not know completely how to get there, at least we know what direction in which we are headed! This keeps us many steps ahead in life and ensures we stay on course. Sometimes as human beings, we do not always know what we need, we just know what we want, but no truth comes from this. This feeling derives from that Self place within us all; has no regard for the real legitimate truth. We must get back to the basics, because problems do not just occur and nothing is left by chance. Everything happens for a reason. Always remember to refer to God's word for guidance. I can guarantee there is some portion of the story in which you can relate, or see yourself in. There is nothing new under the sun, nor the son!

Once we begin to embrace the truth into our lives; then we can simplify our lives by knowing we are protected by The Creator! Life gets easier and simpler with the truth. The reason is because our blessings are automatic when we perceive to live righteously, and there is nothing to think about when we know right from wrong. We base our life's judgments and decisions upon this! We must make it a little easier for The Most High to want to work as it pertains to our interests! Think about it, when we do the wrong things, no one wants to help us because of how we are living. The same thing applies with Our Father

21

who art in Heaven concerning the protection that He provides to the obedient! Our ultimate key and test of survival is "obedience!" Though life is distinctly designed, and the measures can be drastic...we must roll with the punches, but we can make things a little less stressful for ourselves by embracing the truth and stepping outside of falsehood! We must make our peace with ourselves and let everything else of this world go! Once we have begun the process of ejection, direction, and protection, we can then begin our journey to a life of simplicity! This is the process in which every spiritual being must undergo. Remember once we have put down the things from which bring about darkness and begin to see through the light, God can then begin to direct our paths. We must gird up, or protect ourselves through The Holy Spirit, which only comes from the knowledge of our Creator! It is time for us all to step aside from our worldly selves, that is what a child of God could never be!

# "Yesterday Preparation For, Today, Preparation For Tomorrow"

The more we begin to study and observe the course that we are taking, the more we will begin to gain common sense, and or, our insight of noticing the patterns that have been laid out for our lives! These patterns are designed, specifically to help us see the connections between where we have been, where we are now, and where we are headed! We as human beings are not always able to foresee these things, or to understand the patterns that have been designed to reveal what makes our lives our own. We must begin to live in the spirit of God and not flesh of our wombs. Remember the flesh is weak and susceptible to many things. It has been bruised, abused, punctured, and even altered, by self, but not the spiritual self which is selfless! This consistent battle that keeps us consistently battling our own selves is that which it is because we have, with our own free will chosen to be without understanding. Once we begin to gain this spiritual insight that allows us to understand how each day has prepared us for the next, then living, no matter the adversity, will get simpler for us all!

Sometimes in life all we see is what we have been, where we have been, or what we have done in our past, but the true test of our character is to focus in on the lens looking ahead and to make the most through what we have been provided. People oftentimes focus too much on this "past portion" of life, instead of trying to understand what the lesson to be learned might be. This way one can grow from one point to the next. What this does, if we do not sharpen our discerning lens, is creates a cycle for similar mistakes to occur. The key is to prepare the Spiritual You for whatever may occur tomorrow, and not to dwell on any day, but to take something greater that you learned from yesterday and apply it to today to lead you past the point of understanding you had yesterday. If it be that a situational occurrence shall occur, let one not make the same mistakes.

Today is to be seized, and to be made the most of. If ever we have an opportunity to be better, to do something better, or to reveal a speech that is better; we should take the opportunity to grasp a hold and do so. Tomorrow is that of which is not promised, and each day is young. There is no growth in any individual who does not work at an upward angle. If we allow personal feelings to set in front of truth and spiritual growth, we will always remain the same, even throughout the physical changes. We have then allowed the feeling that led us to where we are to conquer and set in on the understanding of where we were headed. One can defeat them self, or one can teach them self to reach them self through the Power and Spirit of The Highest! If we work the nerves that strike curiosity and ingeniousness, we will oftentimes be able to see exactly what our Creator has done, is doing, or why certain things occur in our lives and how one thing connects to another in an only God way preparative for the next stage in our lives, be it for today or for tomorrow.

What is to come, or tomorrow, so to speak, is something that is quite hard to speak on. As it something that has not come every day, comes, and then, has not come yet again. Tomorrow is the future, and we always have an opportunity to make it better through our own free will. What you do today will ultimately impact your tomorrow. Think about it, when you drink alcohol the night before, you are directly impacted the next day. You may develop a hangover, or just feel drowsy and very sluggish. If you had an argument with someone that you live with and did not resolve it today, tomorrow will more than likely be hectic and filled with disruption. If you fill your spirit with the Most High today and study the Holy Script, your tomorrow will more than likely be filled with the spirit of peace and serenity. How you feed yourself today impacts the way that you will dispose of it tomorrow. It may be a good or bad day, depending on your preparatory methods the day before.

All things have their own way of connecting to one another. This is an on- going cycle. Just as things go out of style and come back around again in a similarly different way. Life is amazing like that, but you have not truly lived until you can understand what you go through and are able to distinguish it all. Do not waste you mind because it could be the difference between dull and bright colors. The way we see things means everything. It is important to try to gain a complete under-standing of all things. Patterns are an especially important part of our understanding the culture of our lives. It allows for brief moments to see what it may be that the Most High is doing with our lives. And how yesterday was preparation for today and today is preparation for tomorrow. These are certain moments when our inner light pops on and off, like having an epiphany. If we keep working on the design of what a good day should be then our tomorrow will ultimately be brighter. This also helps to keep us sharp and our understanding keen. Just try waking up each day and thanking the Highest for another day; that understanding of Him just waking you up this morning will be enough to get you started with a good day. Once you reach a certain understanding, which is what this book is all about, you will be able to understand that no matter what occurs, it is always a good day because of the mercy that Christ has for us. We must practice good behavior to see good results.

# "Good Behavior= Good Results"

Most of the things that occur in our lives occur because of something else occurring beforehand. We oftentimes cause our own mishaps if you honestly think about it. Life is very discerning, and there is much to be taken from it through and through. We must become the better portion of our spiritual selves for the physical self to be impacted by it. The spiritual us is invisible to the outside world until both it and the physical portion of ourselves have become one. We must live like the righteous and spiritual us to become those righteous and spiritual individuals. If we stay prayed up, do good deeds, and exhibit good qualities, then we are preparing ourselves for what good results are to come.

Karma is something that can come back around when you are doing something wrong to someone or cause bad things to happen. Those things tend to come back around full circle. I do not necessarily believe in karma as karma, but I do believe that you reap what you have sown. People must be conscientious about every action that they decide to partake in. With every action comes the decision to do or not to do. We as sinful humans must use our conscious to help us to decipher right from wrong because it is in our nature to do the wrong things. We are naturally rebellious people, but to reform ourselves into everything that our father wants us to be, we must listen to our conscious and respond to it appropriately. God is always there, and although we cannot see him, he gives us signs that allow certain parts of our spiritual instincts to kick in. Our conscious is a connection from our minds to our hearts and our souls, and the spirit transports them. This is what allows the outside world to see what comes from inside, because our spirit carries the truth of the heart, the mind, and the soul outward. We must stay prayed up and meditate on the Torah because the repetitive nature of anything can change something. The most important thing to remember is that the days we commit to focusing on truth reveal obedience in time. Progress can be displayed through time, or additional days of dedication that we commit to something that is right. Staying prayed up is our communication with The Highest and we can all administer to his Holy Word. But for the communication with our Father to truly work we must be in-tune with Him, and it is impossible to do so when we are in-tune with everything else of this world. We must let go of everything of this world. The Bible tells us to ask, and we shall receive, but the problem is that most people do not honestly believe. When asking The Highest for something, you cannot have an ounce of doubt inside of you. You must know it and claim it. We must trust in our Holy Father with everything inside of us. Meditating day and night, night and day on his Torah with the help of our imaginations will get us all what we truly desire in this world. If we can perceive it, then we must be prepared to receive it. We oftentimes miss out on our blessings because we lack belief. If we did believe, we would be steadfast and unmovable. God already knows our solutions, but if we maneuver too soon on our own, we run the risk of missing what God has for us.

We also receive blessings when we help others, educate those without the knowledge that we may have, and speak with a pleasant tongue. Oftentimes, we curse ourselves because of the evil that we speak and display to the world. Think good and good will occur, do good and good shall be done unto you. Each person has a duty to be a better humanitarian. We owe it, not only to The Highest and our loved ones, but to ourselves as well to be better people. Love covers a multitude of sins. Doing good deeds is necessary for our personal growth in life. We get nowhere fast by being selfish individuals. This is the way the world works, and there is a process to it. Unfortunately, the way the world is set-up, we must cross the path of another individual to get where we are trying to go most times. There will always be someone with more expertise than you at the gate that you are trying to enter. This is the reason we must work together. People of this world cross-train one another. The Most High placed everyone here with certain strengths and weakness that make us who we are, where we lack strength someone else may pick up or be able to show us the way. We are all pieces to the puzzle of life, and we fit together a certain way. We gain blessings through the good deeds that we do for one another, but we should not necessarily look for a blessing; we should do these things from the heart. This is how we build on our own personal character.

Exhibiting good qualities will almost always get you great results in life. Just as a smile requires a smile back, a good gesture requires a good gesture in return. Thing is, we need to get in the habit of doing good things for people all the time. Just because it is the right thing to do. When we do good things for people, we ultimately feel good about ourselves. This is the biggest reward of all, and although the Most High does bless people for doing good things, we should not necessarily expect this. This way we are not upset with ourselves for doing good for others, because there may not always be anything in it for us besides the satisfaction that doing good to others brings. The goal of life in general is building, no matter what it pertains to.

# "Self -Worth"

To what do we owe one's company? Why does the visitation of an individual always end in the distribution of ourselves in some sort of way? People have a way of being manipulative in nature. Somehow our issues become the issues of the rest of the world, or at least to those who open themselves up to our world's. We all have issues, and some people were created to deal with the issues of random individual's and have a career in doing so. For those who do not, understand that it is still a natural trait to counsel. We do this without an attempt. Most individuals can see exactly what others need to do with their lives but cannot correct their own lives. We cannot point the finger at the next individual because we all do this. And quite frankly it seems like the natural way to do things. It is a part of life, but how do we keep ourselves from being completely affected by this. How do we separate the problems of others from our own personal lives and remain? These sorts of dealings can determine our feelings, our energy, the overall way that our day can turn out, or the way that we deal with the next individual we meet. There is a way to deal with these things, but we must first stop being moved by everything of this world if we desire to be moved by God.

It starts with knowing your self worth, knowing who you are and standing for your individual life's purpose. To understand your individual self-worth, you must look at your culture, you must look at your environment, you have to evaluate yourself ethically and understand your personal values in relation to the values of the world surrounding you. Depending on your faith, you may want to refer the scripture in terms of understanding the covenant made by the Lord, between He and Abraham. God promised to multiply his people exceedingly, he chose us to be his people and He, our God. That alone sets us apart from the Gentile nations. One, this allows us the insight into how much God truly values his people and therefore allows one to think more highly of self, feeling a sense of duty. No matter what the world may experience, it does not impact your personal experience of the goodness, mercy, and glory of the Lord. We know that it was written in the scripture that Abraham's people would endure slavery and affliction for four-hundred years. However, we cannot base self-worth, on how others view us and we certainly cannot base it on what others attempt to do to us. People have personal issues with themselves, and life is a big window for them to witness all their mistakes through. When people do not love themselves, or are not happy with themselves, they will oftentimes take it out on you. We know there are people out here that do not have a covenant with God, and we can tell who God's people truly are based on what the scripture tells us. Not only that, but it is certainly harder for the vast minority of God's people to be successful in this world ran by Gentiles who follow heathenistic ways. Remain loyal to God and to yourself, and always try to reflect Him. Remain royal, be kind, gentle, humble, and meek and watch your value and self-worth increase.

# "OPENING UP OURSELVES"

I t is imperative that we begin to open ourselves up to one another. Our lives and the lives of those surrounding us depend on it. We do not always have to appear to be so tough; closed off or set apart from one another. It is ok to open every once and again. It is ok to be vulnerable in terms of love. Not a one of us knows what we are doing when we first start loving anyway. It is ok to feel the emotions that you truly feel in those moments when they arise. It is ok to live, experience and to go through your different feelings and emotions.

If we would begin to bring what we feel more to the forefront, rather than pushing this to the back, then we would begin to properly deal with the emotions that we feel whenever they choose to arise. We, humans live so closely compacted and oftentimes, we just need a way to release all that we feel and are going through emotionally. Many of us harbor these unre- leased feelings and emotions on the inside of us. Many of us, because we are human, just do not know how to release these emotions, or where to begin. Releasing these emotions sooner has a greater return on your body and letting go of unresolved emotions will later cause one to erupt.

This world has always offered woman more room to express herself, but as a man in this world it is frowned upon to exhibit emotional behavior. The truth is that all humans are all emotionally embedded creatures. We can not help it, whether man or woman. It is ok to express oneself so do not let anyone tell you otherwise, because the suppression of these emotions will lead to greater issues down the line. We as humans must self-express; this always helps us to understand ourselves better as well. It allows us the opportunity to gaze into ourselves and not only see what we feel, but also to be able to evaluate those emotions.

As parents, it is also important to allow our children to be expressive. The more children feel, the more they can open to you, it makes for a better relationship between the parent and child. Children must know that their safe haven is at home and not in the streets with people who may use that information against them. It is a cold world. If a child can not feel secure at home, then they will never find security anywhere else.

# "Manifestation By Staying The Course"

The universe has its very own way of rewarding every individual of this world by allowing their works to manifest the future that lies ahead for them. Whatever a human has their hands in will someday reward them for all their efforts, whether good or bad. That is the catch. You see, for some this can be a very scary thought. There are a lot of individuals of this world whose hands produce nothing but bad fruit. Then there are some who are manifesting a life that is good through their positive attributions to the world. Those individuals will bear nothing but good fruit, and that good fruit will bear more good fruit. The bad apples have become so great in number and the good apples have become so few. Once we realize the power we have over our very own desires, the more we can begin to step in and take the control back over our lives. I am certain that we would much rather have the control than to give it to another individual, or to just allow things to fall where they may.

You see there is a superpower deep within us all, but we need to discover for ourselves what that is. And because we have given so much power over ourselves away, we must find a way to take it back. We must stop basing our lives decisions on how they will affect the rest of the world. How others are affected does matter, but we must always keep ourselves primary concerning all things that pertain to oneself. So, it is imperative that we always remember that we are the source of all things concerning our lives. Self-preservation is the first rule of nature. We all need to practice living primary again and in doing so all things concerning us will begin to fall into their proper places. Things meant to attach to you will, and the things that are not meant to attach will not. This task is easy for some and extremely difficult for others. But we all have our strong points, and believe it or not, a lot of individuals of this world are selfless beings.

It is in a caring one's heart to naturally put others before oneself, but we must always be the source as it pertains to us. When we give too much of this away, we will begin to lose the control that we possess over our own lives. Many people will dim your light if they see you shining harder than them, but just stay the course because what God has for you is only for you. And it is ok to give a little because no candle loses its very own light just by lending that light to another candle. Just be aware of those in it with you versus those in it for only themselves.

For some reason many of us have turned the discernment off; we have turned the intuition off. Everyone seems to be going against their better judgement. Some situations have us wondering if we are making the right decisions, but rather than correct this we follow through with the chaos in our lives. We knew it, we felt it, but for some odd reason we just could not follow through. We must stay the course in our own lives, because what is for our family and our friends or associates is not what is right for our own lives. We should never go against our better judgement, because when something does not feel right then it is not. A lot of the trouble in our lives stems from going against our gut feelings. The gut is right where the soul is and ultimately is where our truth resides.

Typically, the intuition is never incorrect, but following it can be difficult when those pure thoughts are surrounded by one's own personal thoughts and or emotions. The personal ideals are the very thing that throws the truth off from being just what it is, the truth. Our personal feelings and emotions also keep us from receiving the truth. Oftentimes, we humans just need to get out of our own way. Time is the one thing we can never re-retrieve nor can we re-new it. We just must practice a little more efficiency and learn to work smarter rather than harder. One thing about consistency is that it will someday reward itself, we just must stay on the course and everything that we desire will manifest itself.

# "Forgiveness"

When we forgive others, we receive all our power back that holding onto a grudge possesses, and we gain all our strength back from people in our own lives. But when we hold on to things then we tend to harbor the pain that extends from it, whereas pain is guaranteed to weaken any individual. This is a fact, and until we learn to forgive then we will never be able to truly live. We have lived far too long holding on to pain caused by people and things of this world, and it is time to forgive so that we can release it. Think of it like everywhere you travel you are carrying this heavy weight on your back or shoulders. But if you put it down and release it then you can maneuver around a lot easier and without the pain caused by the weight weighing you down. Ultimately excess baggage stagnates your progress and development and holds you up from receiving the blessing that God has set aside for you.

It takes so much more strength to hold onto something, rather than just let it go. So, we must begin to apply this concept to our lives. There can also be no hypocrisy concerning forgiveness. The way we desire forgiveness from others we have committed sins against, we too must forgive others who have mishandled us. This works the same way a two-way street works; both sides of the road are operable. People only hold a power over us that we have given to them when we choose not to forgive one another. The more of you, you keep for you the more whole of an individual you are. The more we piece ourselves off to the rest of the world, lending emotions or too much of our thoughts, the more we become dust or particles that are hard to put back together again. We should only distribute ourselves to those that reciprocate and give something back to us in return; they make us feel fulfilled in our dealings with them. When we deal with only individuals who are not whole themselves, we find ourselves distributing pieces of ourselves to fulfill themselves. When we enter relationships, we need to all be whole individuals, otherwise an imbalance will be created. It is highly unlikely that you will find an individual who is whole these days because we all struggle with something in life. All we can do is love one another despite the things that we may dislike and work with everyone on a case-by-case basis.

The more patience we have the better in this life. We always seem to over distribute ourselves in one way or another. Most individuals whom we over distribute to never return anything back, and so without forgiveness we never replenish ourselves. We never renew our energy tied up in these situations until we forgive as well. When we release; we grow. And when we grow, we re- develop so there is no need for fragments or pieces of the old us. We can do without those old portions of ourselves, they are useless because we have outgrown them, and they no longer fit the new people we have become.

## "THE GREATEST LOVE OF ALL"

We as humans have created a lot of emptiness for ourselves, and so it seems that we have a lot of voids to be
filled. But it would take millions of years and experiences to
complete the task. The only way we can truly be fulfilled is by
receiving the greatest love of all; the love we receive from God
and his only begotten Son. God did not miss one part of this life
we live, he thought about it all and he covered it all. No matter
what we go through in life, our solution can always be a simple
one. However, so many people are afraid of coming into God's
love because they are afraid of the order that comes with it. His
loving mercy is reserved for those who do the will He set forth.
A mother or father is defined by their DNA, and so it the same
concerning our Heavenly Father. If we wish to be children of
the Highest, then we must exhibit some of his qualities.

The love we seek from the world always comes with a price,
but with God's love Christ already paid that price with his life
for us. You see loving someone truly takes a lot of energy if
you are loving the right way. Because in true love, you can see
its benefits. And yes, love should be beneficial. Because loving
someone takes an excess amount of emotion and excess energy,
it should benefit the ones involved. Loving God benefits us
greatly. One thing about it, God never treats us the way we

deserve to be treated. If that were the case, no one would like the actions of God towards them. We all want to experience an un-failing love, but many times we take God's love for granted.

The flip side to all this is that we must also learn to remain consistent in God's life just as he remains consistent in ours. When the world lets us down, God's love remains consistent in our lives. We must delight ourselves in God's love to truly reap the benefits from it, and not make serving God seem like it is a chore, when in fact it is a privilege. 1 John 4:18 states "There is no fear in love, but perfect love cast out fear; because fear hath torment, he that fear is not made perfect in love." We learn the more we live that many things and people often change, but God's love for us remains the same. We must flip the coin on the other side sometimes so we can see how we possibly make God feel with the actions we take along our course. Just as much as we need God, our God needs us also. And it is ok to ask God what you can do for him today. You never know how pleased the Lord will be with you, and the type of blessings you will receive by showing God your heart.

# "Allowing God's Calibration To Happen"

W e as humans will drive ourselves insane trying to figure
out what God is doing in our lives. Therefore, peace
is one of our greatest assets of all once we acquire it, but it
does not come easy. It is difficult to acquire peace amidst our
environment when we are faced with so many circumstances,
but this is only because we do not understand that peace is an
internal mechanism. We cannot achieve peace from this world
or any individual of it. Every one of us needs to practice self-
care and loving on ourselves, meditation and becoming one
with the nature surrounding us. In doing these things, one can
achieve a peaceful state. We just must remember to remain in it.
Keep these good habits going and they will help you to achieve
this permanently.

When we commit our lives to one-ness and whole-ness, we can
process life a whole lot better. This will also allow us to breathe
from the outside world and all its distractions. It will allow us
to hear God's voice and receive the discernment needed along
our journeys. As we mobilize about throughout this contami-
nated world, we must find ways to survive, as well as ways to
thrive. Considering there are many forces against us as well,
our bodies need proper nutrients and adequate rest to properly

function. These habits are crucial to our emotional and mental health. Meditation can also be good to calm one and focus one's spiritual well-being. There are many stresses caused by the outside and inner worlds we reside in, and meditation can help us to ease the anxiety brought on by our expectations in this world. These things hinder our inner peace. All things are made simple in God's eyes, so if we operate in his image and his likeness, then our lives begin to be a little more organized, indicating our internal mess being cleaned up. Cleanliness is next to Godliness so if we clean up our lives messes then we can draw closer to God, creating a simpler life for ourselves through our usage and application of God's eternal law!

It is imperative that we take the time to experience and enjoy our own personal journeys. Sometimes the personal journey to succeed can take a while, but do not be discouraged because the process itself is a beautiful one. That is only contingent upon perception, however. Not enough of us are embracing the process and embracing our struggles. When first accept something, it makes it a lot easier to change it. Each of the struggles we face are specific trials designed for us. If we do not face our trials they will continue to reappear. When we tackle our issues head on, we learn the lesson meant to learn and we can move forward. We tend to learn our strengths and weaknesses the more we experience in this life.

One of the most important lessons we can learn in life is how to walk with God. And not only how to walk with Him, but also how to be in alignment with God along your walk. If our steps align with God in this life, then we will more than likely reach our destinations in our lives. If by some chance our alignment is off with God, then we will run into some issues in along the way. Proverbs 35:5-6 states, "Trust in the Lord with all your heart, and lean not on your own understanding, in all your ways acknowledge him, and he shall direct your paths." When we surrender our own wills for the will of our Lord and Savior, he will reveal his true will for our lives. We just must learn to be receptive to what that is.

It is also good to seek mentorship from those who are following God. They can be valuable to us, in a sense of helping us to discern what that plan is that God has for our lives. Proverbs 11:14 states, "Where there is no counsel the people fall, but in the multitude of counselors there is safety. Knowledge is safety and cushion in this life. It allows us the leverage we need to make vast, but precise decisions as we maneuver throughout our lives. Pay attention to how God has structured you as an individual. What talents and gifts has God provided you with that set you apart from the average person. 1Peter 4:10 says, "As each one has received a gift, minister it to one another, as good stewards of the manifold grace of God." So, we have all be given a specific gift that is special and distinctive to us; these gifts allow us the ability to perform special missions for the Lord. Each in our very own way. We must pay attention and tap into these gifts, because whatever we are the best at is what God has given us to utilize as our specialty. It is the one thing that will give us the best results in our lives. We do not have to study our gifts, because they just exist in us. Let us allow God to calibrate and re-calibrate as needed, because without it we cannot align and re-align ourselves for God to bring out our highest self. In order do this, we must learn to listen to our spirits and our intuition or gut feelings. We cannot always rely on the heart because the heart will lead us astray if we allow it to. Our hearts are led by our emotions and our spirit is guided by God and his eternal logic.

# "BE ANXIOUS ABOUT NOTHING"

Visualize this, the thing in which you wait for is coming, but to it you are coming. As it concerns you, you are going, but to it you are also leaving. When I speak of leaving, I am speaking of leaving the body. The body is only equipped enough to handle the calm. The reason is because the calm fits easily within us. Anytime our spirit is over-excited, the spirit leaves the body. Anything more than the body's usual calm will be too much to reside in the body. This pertains to both good and bad in our lives. For instance, when the spirit is delighted in the Lord, and is over-joyed in the Lord, we call this the Holy Spirit. The spirit comes out of the body and no longer belongs to it. Whenever we are too anxious about something, the spirit of excitement leaves the body and departs somewhere else once the thing we are waiting on finally arrives, and is fulfilled.

Imagine being too excited about something too soon, and what you are waiting for is weeks or even months down the line…the anxiousness about the situation is going to cause you a great deal of anxiety. We should never get our hopes up too high in any situation because you never know how plans will truly turn out when life takes its course. Philippians 4:6-7 states, "Do not be anxious about anything, but in everything, by prayer and petition, with thanksgiving present your requests to God. And peace of God, which transcends all understanding will guard your hearts and minds in Christ Jesus." This is what God's word tells us. The fears that we face in our lives mostly concern our past, but the things that we are anxious about concern our future. We cannot access either of those time capsules. The past will worry about itself, and the future will take care of itself. We only utilize the memories of the past to bring forth a better future. Yesterday serves as our preparation for today and today serves as our preparation for tomorrow. Tomorrow has yet to arrive, so it does us no good to worry about it, especially considering we must still make it through this very day.

When we focus too much ahead, we tend to miss the "Now." The now concerns the things right in front of us that we tend to look over when we focus too much on other time capsules that are out of our control. In the now, we run the risk of missing opportunities that present themselves throughout the day and miss the opportunity to seize the valuable time we spend with our loved ones. The things right in front of us require our eye now so we must slow down enough to feel everything, and to discern everything. We miss out on a lot by being currently unavailable. You know mentally unavailable, spiritually unavailable; when your mind just is not in the now, but rather stuck focusing on things of the past that we could not change if we wanted to. We should start every single day with a grateful mindset to set the tone for our day. If we do this, we will act in love more and from a place of appreciation for life and the fact that God saw fit to wake us up yet again. It also allows us to reassure ourselves that there is someone greater and higher than ourselves that controls the day. God ultimately controls the way things go. This will allow us to self-correct and humble ourselves, so we are less likely to go out into the world and crash out.

# "VISIONS FROM GOD"

Visions are the state of being able to see. When I speak of site, let me clarify things by setting the record straight that even those with eyes are blind to the facts of life. There are some blind people who have a better, and more precise vision of life in general. The blind must rely on their imagination to see. This is where those that have eyes go blind. Because the older we that have eyes to see get, the less we perceive and the more the imagination becomes dull and less vivid. Meaning we become less imaginative people the older we get. But remember even faith in God requires the imagination and belief in an omnipotent being who we have never laid eyes on. So many of us still have an imagination we just do not tap into it enough, or our faith is not where we say it is.

God gives us visions and allows us to dream, but we still need our imagination to fully envision our visions and to be totally resourceful beings. Once we lose our imagination, we lose the ability to believe in our God. 2 Corinthians 4:18 says, "As we look not to the things that are unseen. For the things that are seen are transient, but the things that are unseen are eternal." Things of this world are temporary, but God's love and will for our lives is everlasting. Acts 2:17 says, "And in the last days it shall be," God declares, "that I will pour out my spirit on all flesh, and your sons and daughters shall prophesy, and your young men shall see visions, and your old men shall dream dreams."

The more time we spend alone, the more time we must learn and recognize the voice of our God. When he speaks to us, and through the visions that he places in ours we can recognize him. The New Testament as well as the Old Testament speak of an out-pour of spiritual dreaming and visions poured out on God's children. Many of his people are beginning to prophesy, but we must also be aware of false and misleading prophets. God will speak to us through our dreams as a direct revelation concerning something.

Our visions are given to us during our awake state, rather than when we are sleeping like dreams are. Numbers 24:4 speaks of dreams that we dream when we are awake. In the scripture they are referred to as "waking dreams." God will utilize our dreams to also speak to us and through us. He oftentimes, reveals his plans for our lives allowing for us to connect to him, and tap in spiritually. Sometimes, God will use our dreams to warn us of things that could possibly harm us and to provide us with solutions ahead of time.

We must be mindful that if we are always falling asleep intoxicated, and with a clouded mind that we run the risk of missing numerous prophesies that God gives us. God will give us little glimpses into what he is doing regarding our lives. These epiphanies typically are inaccessible until God reveals them to us. But he will use the visions and dreams he provides us with to reveal himself, and to make his presence known in times we may often forget. A lot of times we must slowdown in our course to catch the things God wants to reveal to us, and the things that he is trying to show us in our own lives. Sometimes we must set ourselves apart from any outside distractions; just until we are used to God's presence and used to hearing his voice, which is typically ours in our own minds. This is God speaking through our higher self or consciousness. We must be slow to speak and quick to listen in this life. When we live too loud in color, we can oftentimes attract the wrong attention, but if we live a little more quietly, we can obtain the peace we wish to obtain from God in our lives. Remember everyone cannot know how you move, and not everyone who knows your ambitions is praying for your best...sometimes it is just the opposite, they prey.

# "SOUL TIES"

M any people are lost in the misconception of sex being just that, sex. The truth is every time we lay down with a person, some of the other individual's spirit is left within us, whether good or bad. The more encounters we have as humans, the more soul tie connections are created. So, unless we have spiritually cleansed ourselves with the Lord, we have a bit of every individual we have laid down with inside of us. Oftentimes we face spiritual battles because of this spiritual residue that is left over internally. So, sex is not just sex, it is much deeper than the eye can perceive.

If we look at where God placed our reproductive organs, we will notice that they are discreetly placed for good reason. God created an order for our lives to keep the problems to a minimum. The way he intended for us to structure our lives really was the best thing for humankind. Marriage first, learn your partner and then the act of sex once you know your partner. The bible tells us that the person you give your body to is your wife or your husband. Exodus 22:16 states, "If a man seduces a virgin who is not betrothed and lies with her, he shall give the bride-price for her and make her his wife." So technically, the man who takes your virginity is indeed made your husband, according to God's law. Marriage is a sacred thing in God's eyes. So, when the Lord discreetly placed our organs out of sight, it was his way of saying these organs are sacred and not for everyone's eyes or sinful pleasures.

Soul ties are very real. Most of the research done over the course of time draws the concept of a soul tie back to biblical times. 1 Corinthians 6:15 says, "Do you not know that the one who joins himself to a prostitute is one body with her? For He says, 'The two shall become one flesh.'" So, when we join ourselves with one who prostitutes, or sleeps with multiple partners we then take on all of them. There are big rewards to operating under God's law. The more we go against the grain trying to recreate laws for ourselves, the more issues our lives will bring us. Therefore causing us to be more susceptible to things in this life. When we know better it is an absolute must that we follow through with that. God desired for man and woman to be joined together as one and allow his word to reside within them.

On a more scientific level, limbic bonding, or neurological changes occur in both individual's brains as they engage in sexual intercourse. When you assume you are just having casual sex, it is always more than that. An emotional bond is built between the two individuals, even if they do not know it is occurring. Women have a larger limbic system, and so the bond that women gain is much greater than that of a man. This is what causes women to feel more of a connection after sex, allowing for more hurt. Most often women with strong soul ties suffer great emotional damage, and they do not understand the spiritual soul tie battle that they are facing.

There are ways to reverse soul ties, but it takes an intense building with God on a much deeper spiritual level. We must confess to God the things that need confessing so that he can fix it. If we are not honest with the Lord concerning ourselves, we run the risk of setting up a barrier that prohibits direct communication with God for lack of sincerity. If we want to break a soul tie, we must disconnect from that individual or those individuals whom we have developed that soul tie with. Staying away and unplugging, burning old photos and meditating on who you are will most certainly help.

## "GOD'S NO IS JUST AS IMPORTANT AS HIS YES"

If God were to give us all the sunshine with no rain at all it would not benefit our souls at all. If all we knew was God's yes, it would ruin us. We would forget about God, ultimately. God allows us to see the rain so that we are reminded that there is someone much greater than ourselves, and as a reminder that we still need him in every situation. This reminds us of God's face. We would have no reason to call on God anymore if he always gave us the desires of our hearts. People only tend to call on God when things are going wrong for them, but when everything is good in life God rarely hears from us.

When Satan promised things everlasting, like money and things of this world, he forgot to mention that we would never acquire happiness nor peace with these things. That is the spiritual battle concerning it all. Satan knows that if he gives you all the desires of your heart, that you will begin to forget about God. That is the downfall with a human, we serve whoever we think is benefitting us at the time. We never stop to realize that we have not truly tried God enough to know how his love benefits us.

In the book of Job, we are introduced to an exceptional man in the eyes of God. He was a very prosperous rancher. The scripture tells us that Job's hands were blessed by God and that he had seven sons and three daughters, and although Job was an upright man, he thought his children might somehow offend God by cursing or drunkenness. So, at every feast Job was sure to sanctify his children. God knew Job was a faithful man and he allowed Satan to test him, because Satan thought that Job's devotion to God was only due to him blessing him so greatly. God knew otherwise. During the test, all of Job's livestock died and so did his children. But, although Job lost everything, his faithfulness would not allow him to curse God and he remained blameless. Because of this, God blessed Job exceedingly. He received everything he lost back tenfold

What this teaches us is that sometimes God will test us for his very own purpose to see our level of faithfulness. It is far less about those who talk the talk, and more about those who walk the walk. Always be encouraged and remain faithful to God, because at the end of the day he always has your best interest. God's rain is just as important as his sunshine, God's adversity is just as important as the great times he provides us with, and God's no is just as important as the yes that he gives us. Most times when God tells us no, it is the very thing that saves our lives.

# "THE PRIVILEGE OF PRAYER"

P rayer is our very opportunity to build a bond with God, and a chance to get better in our communications concerning him. This is time invested with God that we need to build a foundation with him. If we always look at the times we pray to God as times of obligations rather than the true privilege it is, then we miss the opportunity to see how meaningful prayer can be to our lives and the lives of others around us. We must remember that we have a Father that wishes to be present in our lives, our God is no dead beat. He wants to walk with us in all that we do in life, but we must want God beside us. As we grow, learn, experience, struggle or whatever it may be, he wishes to walk with us to see us through this journey we call life. So, we are never alone. But every relationship must be nourished, even the one we have with God.

In Philippians 4:6-7 The apostle Paul tells us, "Do not be anxious about anything, but in every situation, by prayer and petition, with thanksgiving, present your request to God. And the peace of God, which transcends all understanding will guard your hearts and minds in Christ Jesus." So, through prayer God can begin to build a relationship of trust with us. The more we speak with God, the more we recognize his voice when he speaks to us. God's responses are to the prayers that his children pray to him. If we develop habits of talking to God, we can ask for what we want, and it shall be given. We are more likely to ask and receive things from one we have taken the time to get to know.

Prayer helps us to remember we are not God and that we are only able to do the things we do because God strengthens us to do so. Through prayer we gain our strength from the Lord. We cannot communicate our feelings to so many others of the world but hold back in our communication with God. We must trust God and not be afraid to walk with him. He is the greatest friend we can have. We Should get inspired by God's word to take the proper steps in faith rather than by site. We must always let our actions reflect one who stands in the face of God. Remember when we know our parents are present, we as children act accordingly. We must act as if we always know our God is present. God is fully aware of our movements, as well as our positioning on every decision we make. He knows our hearts, and so let us get to know God's heart and his love for us truly. In a true relationship, both parties are familiar with the other and so it is so important to communicate with God so we can get to know him on a more intimate level.

# "BE GRATEFUL"

God rewards those with a grateful heart. The world will also reward those with a grateful heart. People are always more likely to do for you when display gratitude, and appreciation for their kind act toward you. Gratitude can measure our level of value for our relationships. It shows the level of quality we perceive from the relationships we have. When appreciate someone, it is necessary to show them that you care for them, and that you are grateful for the things that they attribute to you. When people do not value what you do for them, you will see it through their actions towards you.

Gratitude, the word itself, derives from the Latin word Gratus, meaning to be grateful and pleasing. So, to be grateful is the same as having appreciation in your heart for someone and something. It also means expressing your thankfulness and kindness in return to the people who do for you in your times of need. We must appreciate the little or big things people do for us, because they are not required to lend us a hand. Humans have an issue with feeling entitlement to the possessions of the people we have ties to. This should never be the case. No one owes us a thing. We owe it to ourselves to stand up and provide our own needs. So, when we do not have it and someone lends us a hand, that is a time to be grateful in our hearts.

We must learn to appreciate the simple things in life again. The things that cost nothing to enjoy are usually the most valuable possessions we have in life. Simple pleasures are free and readily available to us all. Things like fresh air, knowledge or information, our family or loved ones, and most importantly our right to a relationship with God are the things that truly matter in life. When we show appreciation for God and the simple things he provides, then we show God that we have a grateful heart. God recognizes these things, and the angels take notes. Because of this, God will either increase us or decrease us. This is all based on the state and condition of our hearts. God rewards his children when they are grateful and when they give with a sincere heart. The true benefit of doing good is just the rewarding feeling we receive from it.

When we please God, we receive peace from it that surpasses all our understanding combined. When we acquire peace in our lives, we must hold on to it because it is one of our greatest assets. With peace being an internal mechanism, we will never acquire it through people or things of this world. But when we do good, we can add more cushion to ourselves; more protection which ultimately causes us to worry less and adds peace to our hearts. We do not benefit ourselves by being ungrateful humans. In fact, we bring a dark cloud over our lives. The result of not appreciating God or anyone else in your life is that they will stop being there for you.

Once you lose good people its hard to get them back. But when you lose God, you lose altogether and that includes his protection for you. The good thing is our God is a forgiving God and his mercy endures forever, all we must do is call on God, repent and change it. Remember also, gratitude is essential in our prayers to God if we really wish to change things in our lives. We must always remind God when we ask things of him, that the things he has already done in our lives have not gone unnoticed and more importantly, have not gone in vain.

# "2 SIDES 2 EVERY STORY"

Perception is what designs the world we live in concerning our personal lives, and the way we view it. If we look more deeply into the concept of perception, it may help us all to be a little more understanding, patient, and kind to one another. Only things that truly exist in our world are the things that we can perceive, or the things we can visualize in our minds. Those are the things that become our beliefs, or the things that are real to us. We each were given one lens to look through. Each lens is motivated by the individual's life, values, and experiences. This is the reason that they vary so greatly. So, what you see is not necessarily wrong, but neither is what another sees. The understanding is just that they differ.

We have all succeeded at something as well as failed at something. Those experiences affect the way we see things after that. We are humans and so every lesson that we have had to learn has taught us something, and everyone learns differently. So, you consider these things, and you say to yourself, "because we learn differently, the way we perceive will also be different." The result of each person's life and input will always be different. Everyone has their own fears and insecurities as well. This changes the perspective as well. With fear comes insecurities where lack of motivation and lack of confidence reside. People who have experienced more failures, tend to see the world as a scary place. Whereas people who have experienced many successes tend to see the world as their very own playground.

Every difference behind our lens tends to filter every life concept through its very own distortions. This causes every individual to believe that what they perceive through there very own lens is being perceived correctly. This is where prideful humans bump heads because the desire is to be right, creates conflict in a shared space. Humans have an issue with accepting that two people can agree to disagree. We must share this world, and it would make maneuvering through it much easier to learn to tolerate the opinions of others. If those opinions do not affect your wellbeing, then it really does not matter. Everyone is entitled to their own lens. That is part of the beauty in the world to be able to see so many diverse people with different mindsets. We learn and grow in life by sharing knowledge, experience, and perspective.

Being right is never worth the loss or exchange of a person. Not everyone can be disposed of in your life for the sake of perspective, because not everyone is replaceable. If we take more time to learn and understand one another then we can all learn to appreciate the fact that there are two sides to every story, and that is ok. Always be willing to listen to the other person because oddly, you never know what you may or may not learn from them. Sometimes our judgements of others run a lot deeper than we even perceive. Oftentimes, we judge others for the exact flaws we see within ourselves. There is so much to take into consideration when considering each human on this earth, because not one of us is the same. We have an opportunity to be many versions of ourselves, but its best we choose to operate in our higher selves.

Let us never hold grudges against one another or charge one another for humanly offenses. None of us are perfect in the eyes of others. We risk losing some of the best people in our lives for holding on to things that just do not matter all that much at the end of the day. There is always a bigger picture, it has just been there so long that people tend to forget it exists and never look at it. With time being our only non-renewable resource, it is so important to value the time we spend together on this earth. Life is short. In life, the only way we reverse the hatred is by loving one another. The bible tells us the love covers a multitude of sins, and so everything breaks down to us just loving one another in simpler form.

## "LOVE IN THE SIMPLEST FORM"

W hen you think about it, everything breaks down to one thing, and that is love. It is life in its simplest form. True love is kind and warm and peaceful. Love knows how to treat you. Love does not create conflict; nor does it reside in it. Love has your best interest at heart and wants the best for you. Love is giving and knows how to conduct itself in and out of your presence. If the world could operate from a place of love, then the world would be a much better place. Just think about it, operating from a place of love would mean that everyone was looking out for the best interest of one another. When you care for a person, you want to see the best for them and all your acts concerning them will benefit them. They will not be acts of manipulation; or acts that attribute you gains from the other person.

The lack of love has attributed to the world being such an unkind place. No one cares anymore, and the world seems to get a kick out of doing all the wrong things. The world recalls lust rather than love. Love has lost its way due to the misuse of its name and its purpose in the world. We must get back to the original way. If all things were removed from mankind, we would be forced to see our lives for what they were, and we would get in survival mode. Ultimately, causing us to learn to rely on one another to make it. Also resulting in more pure hearts because we all would be in the same boat. This would cause us to understand what one another was going through, resulting in a real love and more compassion for one another.

The problem with the world today is that it has lost its compassion for its brethren. We cannot turn the cheek and watch our loved ones suffer any longer, especially if we are able to provide a way for others. The goal is to love and educate one another. Share resources because we must share this world. God is love and his love for us has always be unfailing. We should utilize it more. Love will heal the world.

To my readers,

Thank you for taking the time to consider this spiritual truth. My goal with this book was to not only educate us in various areas of life, but also to build with every individual one by one as they read the information provided. I hope I was able to pierce the heart that would receive this knowledge that God has bestowed on me throughout this journey we call life. Part of God's vision for each of is to share our gifts and knowledge with the world. That is how we build and spread love, knowledge, and awareness. There was no one of our generation who had observed, taken notes, and written about what they had seen, for others to gain comprehension of how this life works. God placed it on my heart to do so. So, as we take this journey together, please spread the messages that I have shared with you and placed on your hearts, and together we can begin to make the world a better place by just simply beginning with ourselves. This is just the beginning…

Thank You,
Aa'shia D. Jackson
Ai'scei Gold'n Babei

CPSIA information can be obtained
at www.ICGtesting.com
Printed in the USA
LVRC080823110821
694919LV00021B/1